CARS

CORVETTE

Michael Bradley

Marshall Cavendish
Benchmark
New York

Marshall Cavendish Benchmark
99 White Plains Road
Tarrytown, NY 10591-5502
www.marshallcavendish.us
Copyright © 2009 by Marshall Cavendish Corporation

All Internet sites were available and accurate when sent to press.

Library of Congress Cataloging-in-Publication Data

Bradley, Michael, 1962—
The Corvette / by Michael Bradley.
p. cm. — (Cars)
Includes bibliographical references and index.
ISBN 978-0-7614-2976-0
1. Corvette automobile—Juvenile literature. I. Title. II. Series.
TL215.C6B73 2009
629.222'2—dc22 2007024631

Photo research by Connie Gardner

Cover photo by Ron Kimball/www.kimballstock.com

The photographs in this book are used by permission and through the courtesy of: *Alamy*: Transtock Inc., backcover, 24; *Ron Kimball/www.kimballstock.com*: 1, 19, 20, 26(T), 27(T), 29; *AP Photo*: 13,15; General Motors, 4; Darron Cummings, 8; Miranda Pederson, 16; Ron Edmonds, 28; *Corbis*: Car Culture, 5, 9(T),10; Reuters/Mike Blake, 6; John Sommers, 7; Lucas Jackson, 27(B); *Getty Images*: Car Culture, 9(B), 25; Time and Life Pictures, 21; *The Image Works*: National Motor Museum/HIP, 14; *GM Archive*: 23, 26(B).

Publisher: Michelle Bisson
Art Director: Anahid Hamparian
Series Designer: Daniel Roode

Printed in Malaysia
1 3 5 6 4 2

CONTENTS

CHAPTER ONE

AN AMERICAN CLASSIC

The 1953 Corvette is one of the ten most influential vehicles of the last fifty years, according to the influential *Consumer Reports* magazine.

The others have come and gone. **Muscle cars**. **Concept cars**. The Edsel.

But the Corvette remains. For more than fifty years, it has been America's sports car, and drivers love its speed and cool looks. The Corvette was introduced in 1953, but it's definitely not old and tired. Just hit the gas, and you'll hear it come to life.

The 1953 Corvette's back end looked like no other—nor did its entire body, created out of fiberglass by General Motors designer Harley Earl.

5

The Corvette's power and style are unique, just as America is unlike any other country in the world. Corvette owners are proud of their cars. They hold on to them for years. Decades. One man was even buried in his Corvette. To these satisfied people, the Corvette isn't just a sharp piece of transportation, it's a way of life.

Each year, thousands flock to Bowling Green, Kentucky, the site of the National Corvette Museum, to celebrate the car. They visit the museum, talk with other enthusiasts, buy all sorts of gadgets, and just enjoy owning America's top sports car.

The Corvette has a rich and impressive history. It began when General Motors (GM) was looking to challenge Ford and European automobile makers. At the time, the big name in sports cars was the Jaguar XK120, which was made in Great Britain. That car cost too much for the average American driver. So, the Corvette was born. Now it's

Joe Novak's Corvette wasn't around on December 7, 1941, when Pearl Harbor was attacked, but it is not much younger. Both Pearl Harbor survivor Novak and his antique Corvette were going strong at the San Diego Veterans Day Parade on November 11, 2002.

a powerhouse that looks so good, people can't stop staring. If you want power, the Corvette is for you. Slip behind the wheel, and it's hard to tell whether you're driving a car or taking off in an airplane. Pure driving excitement has always been the goal.

The Corvette has been the **pace car** at the Indianapolis 500, and why not? America's top automobile race should be led by America's top sports car. Throughout the years, the Corvette has always been a **prowling**, low-to-the-ground machine that has been just plain cool to drive. Whether in its **convertible** or hardtop form, the Corvette has always attracted attention. When it was introduced in 1953, Chevrolet sent the first fifty cars to entertainers and sports stars, figuring America's idols would want to be seen in a sharp automobile. Stars still drive the Corvette, but so can everybody else. And drivers always look good behind the wheel.

This 1957 Corvette Roadster is only one of many on display at the National Corvette Museum in Bowling Green, Kentucky.

Former Indianapolis 500 winner Johnny Rutherford rides in the passenger seat as former Secretary of State Colin Powell gets ready to drive the Corvette that was the official pace car at the eighty-ninth Indianapolis 500 on May 29, 2005.

When the hood pops open, **mechanics** and hot-rodders always want to have a look at the powerful engine that makes the Corvette go. It's strong enough for a tank, but it isn't hard to handle. It's almost like the car knows just what the driver wants to do. Each new model has more impressive options

A look at the engine of a 1963 Corvette Grand Sport!

than the last. Though it's hard to top the cutting-edge look of the classic Corvettes from the 1960s, today's version still gets people excited.

There are plenty of other sports cars out there, and each has its own personality. But the Corvette remains in its own class, thanks to its tradition, unequaled style, and remarkable power. It has come a long way since 1953, but in many ways it remains the same car. It is **sleek** and beautiful. And it is uniquely American.

The 1957 Corvette was uniquely American in look—and as thrilling as a ride on a roller coaster.

The 1957 Corvette convertible featured an updated, supercharged engine that made the car into the popular legend it is today.

It was made of **fiberglass**, not steel. That was the first sign that this new Chevrolet was something special. Cars weren't made of fiberglass in 1953. Fiberglass was too light. But since Chevrolet needed something to make young people take a look at its new car, it took a chance.

So, Harley Earl, the design chief for General Motors (Chevrolet was a division of GM) built a sports car that looked a bit like the Jaguar XK120. He had tried the same thing before with two other cars, but it didn't work out. Then someone asked him a question: "Why don't you make something that you can race?" So he did.

The name Corvette was taken from World War II ships that rescued people at sea and patrolled the waves looking for enemies. This car wouldn't do anything that heroic, but its name certainly attracted attention. When it was introduced at the 1953 Chicago Auto Show, the largest show of its kind, the Corvette was a sensation. The white car with the black convertible top may not have been as powerful as the Jaguar, but it sure looked good. Chevrolet thought it could challenge the Ford Thunderbird for the title of America's Hottest Sports Car.

The problem was it cost too much, at least at first. At $3,500, it was $200 more than the Jaguar. And the Jag traveled from 0 to 60 miles per hour (0 to 96.5 kilometers per hour)—a second quicker than the Corvette—and went 25 mph (40 km/h) faster. What's worse, the car had no top and leaked water. Though people crowded into dealerships to get a look, only three hundred Corvettes were made. Many of those went to celebrities and star athletes who could afford the hefty price (for 1953). When folks made it to showrooms, the Corvette wasn't always available. And when they saw one, they couldn't afford it.

But Chevrolet wasn't about to give up. Two years later it sold 675 of the 700 Corvettes it made. Who cared if Ford sold 16,155 Thunderbirds? This was progress! By 1958 the car was restyled, and in 1963 the **Stingray** model was introduced to cheers and rave reviews. By now, Chevrolet had a different problem: too many people wanted the Corvette, and they were ready to buy one. Even though a **coupe** was introduced—before then, Corvettes had only been available as convertibles— there still weren't enough for everybody who wanted one.

Corvettes and sports! Quaterback Johnny Unitas of the Baltimore Colts was awarded one of the first—this 1958 roadster was given to him by *Sports* magazine for his outstanding performance in a title playoff game.

The Stingray was introduced in 1963 to raves from fans. By 1969, when this model was produced, sales were climbing as fast as the Stingray could race.

As the 1960s rolled on, the Corvette became more powerful. On November 7, 1969, the 250,000th Corvette—a gold convertible—rolled off the **production line** in St. Louis, Missouri. In the 1970s it remained a powerhouse. Sales grew, and the car became faster and sharper in appearance. Highlights of the 1980s included moving the plant where the Corvette was built from St. Louis to Bowling Green. In 1987 the Corvette became the Indy 500 pace car, leading the drivers around the track before the race began. One year later, the National Corvette Museum was founded in Bowling Green.

Plenty of other sports cars were built during the 1990s, but Corvette continued to thrill American drivers. New, more powerful models stood tall against competitors at home and overseas. On July 2, 1992, the one-millionth Corvette was produced. During the next ten years, Corvette's design looked a bit like the original. But it was never a car from the past. Corvette continued to face the future.

In 1992, the one-millionth Corvette rolled off the production line!

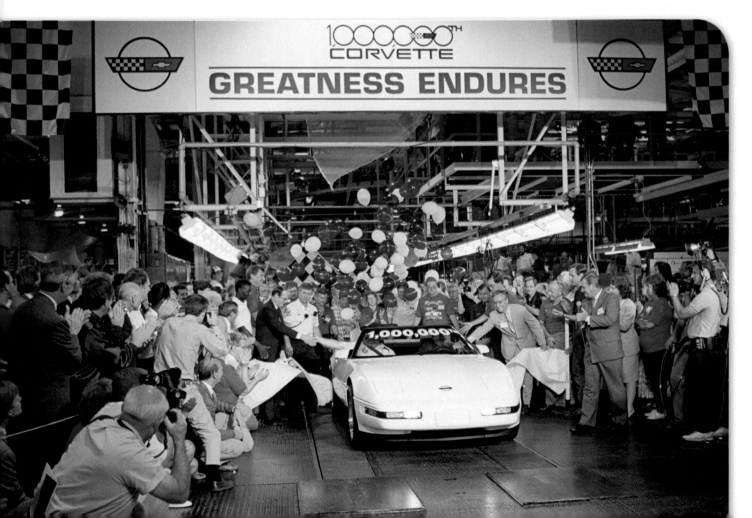

The Corvette had a look like no other car, from its smiling grill to its sleek body.

CHAPTER THREE
THE LOOK OF A CLASSIC

In the beginning it was about imitating the classics. The Corvette copied the Jaguar a little bit. Then, it looked like a Mercedes. Finally, it began to develop its own personality.

And what a personality it was.

Before long, the Corvette looked like nothing else, and nothing else looked like a Corvette. In 1956 the Corvette got a new body. Then, in 1958, Chevrolet came out with a model that had four headlights and a wide-open **grill** that looked almost as if the car was smiling. Over the next five years, it became more sleek and sharp. But the real surprise came in 1963 when the Stingray was introduced.

It was unlike anything America had ever seen. Low to the ground and looking almost like a prowling animal, it featured Corvette's first hardtop. And that top had a surprise—a split rear window. Though some worried that the bar in the middle of the rear window wasn't too safe, it was clearly different. And different was what Corvette was all about.

The split rear window lasted only a couple years, but the Stingray remained a favorite. After the model was introduced, Corvette sales grew quickly. Throughout the 1960s the Stingray improved every year.

When the 1970s began the Stingray was still the main Corvette model. Of course, there were some variations. A Mako Shark model emerged in 1969 that looked so much like the big fish that it almost wasn't allowed near the beach. A Manta Ray version was low to the ground, like the winged swimmer.

The 1970s featured constant improvements to the Corvette's powerful engine, along with a lot of body changes. The car continued to have the long front end and was kept low to the ground. In 1978 the Corvette celebrated its twenty-fifth **anniversary** by becoming the official pace car of the Indianapolis 500. The resulting model, with its special paint job and Indy 500 stickers, was expensive—but worth it.

The 1963 Stingray featured a split rear window. The design didn't last long, but the car became a classic collector's item.

By 1983 the Corvette had undergone a big change. The shark design that had debuted in 1968 was gone, replaced by a car that had a much different look. The back window was larger. The hood opened away from the driver like a clamshell.

And, like the Stingray, there were different versions. In 1988, famous designer Reeves Callaway created a twin-**turbo** model that went from 0 to 60 mph (0 to 96.5 km/h) in a remarkable 4.6 seconds. The LT5 was a smaller Corvette but still quite powerful.

Stingray's Shark line only increased Corvette's reputation as having amazing sports cars like none the United States had ever seen. This 1964 Shark I sits on the sand of a beach.

The ZR1 model cost $50,000 and featured a longgggggggggg front end—three-quarters of the entire car.

The ZR1 kept everybody happy in the early 1990s, but people were looking forward to the fortieth anniversary model, which was scheduled to be released in 1993. It didn't make it to showrooms until 1997, but it was worth the wait. The car was wider and lower. It featured rounded front and rear ends that looked like a Corvette from the 1960s. The sixth-generation Corvette was introduced in 2005, looking more than ever like the old days, but still with plenty of twenty-first century features.

And still looking good. Of course.

21

CHAPTER FOUR

UNDER THE HOOD

Corvette fans have always been excited about the car's unique look, but the big story is under the hood. That's where the promise of power becomes a reality.

From the moment it was created, the Corvette was going to be fast. Really fast. When your role models are Jaguars and Mercedes, you want to produce more than a little speed. The first Corvette hit the road in 1953 with a six-**cylinder** engine called the Blue Flame Special. It went from 0 to 60 mph (0 to 96.5 km/h) in 11 seconds. Its top speed of 105 mph (169 km/h) was pretty swift. But it wasn't swift enough. Other cars moved even faster.

The 1953 Corvette hit the road with the Blue Flame Special six-cylinder engine.

22

The LS1 V-8 engine was one of the most powerful on the road!

Two years later the Corvette had a V-8 (eight-cylinder) engine that made it to 60 mph (96.5 km/h) in eight seconds and could go 120 mph (193 km/h). Even though buyers didn't get too excited, mechanics and others who liked to work on cars were thrilled. They loved the Corvette's power. There was so much interest among them that Chevrolet began to create special models for racing. In 1956 a 240-**horsepower** model won Corvette's first Sports Car Club of America national racing title.

In the 1960s the Corvette continued to get stronger and stronger. Its horsepower output grew to 435. That was well above the average car. Chevrolet also introduced a four-wheel **suspension**, which allowed drivers to control the Corvette better while traveling at top speeds.

In 1965 Corvette started using four-wheel **disk brakes**. This brake system allowed for more reliable stopping, especially if the car was moving fast.

As the motor became more powerful, the unique fiberglass body grew sleeker, and the car's speed increased. Now, it could reach 60 mph (96.5 km/h) in under six seconds. And with each new model year came special editions that could almost fly. In 1967 Corvette introduced an engine option—the L88—that was so powerful, it ran at

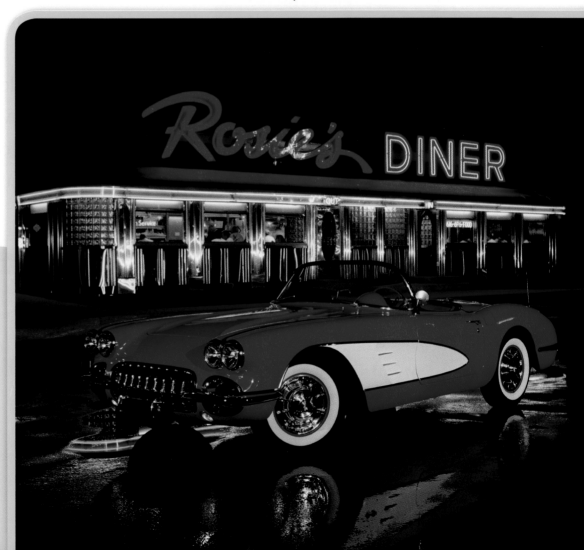

Many consider the 1960s the golden age of the Corvette. This 1960 model combines the curving grace of the 1950s models with the forward motion of the 1960s to come.

In 1967 Corvette introduced the L88 engine. This 1969 Stingray shows just how cool the late 1960s cars looked.

almost 560 horsepower. It was so strong, it almost wasn't allowed on the street, just on the race track.

Many consider the late 1960s and early 1970s the golden age for performance cars like the Corvette. Because the government wasn't forcing carmakers to build engines that didn't **pollute** the air so much, the companies could do whatever they wanted to produce more power. Chevrolet created varieties of its Corvette Stingray that almost flew. One was the ZL1, which came close to 600 horsepower. The Z version still exists today in a super-fast coupe model.

Throughout the 1980s and 1990s, the Corvette continued to get faster—and to introduce special models. In 1987 Corvette introduced the Callaway Twin-Turbo, a two-**exhaust** car that

The L88 V-8 test engine.

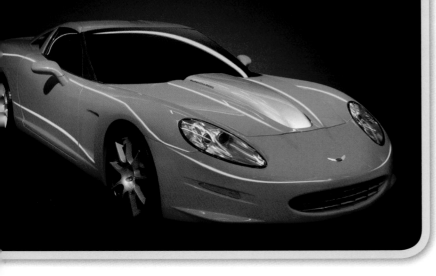

The 2007 Corvette Callaway C16 Coupe has a supercharged 616 bhp engine and 582 lb.-ft. of torque.

really moved. By 1989 the LT5 featured a six-speed transmission that allowed it to blaze down the road. And when the ZR1 showed up in 1990, Chevrolet had almost produced a rocket ship.

The Z line continued through the 1990s and into the twenty-first century. The standard Corvette coupe was still fast and sharp. But the car's real fans were looking for something extra. The Z line gave them that. They wanted more power and were interested in a model that could challenge the fastest cars from Europe and Japan. The Corvette was more than up to the challenge—just as it had always been.

And always will be.

The Z06 car debuts at the 2006 auto show. The official pace car of the 2006 Indianapolis 500 was driven by talk show host Jay Leno.

1953 Corvette Roadster

Special Fact:

Only 300 were produced

150 hp
Engine Size: 238 ci/3.9L
Engine Type: Blue Flame 6-cylinder
Weight: 2,703 lbs (1,226 kg)
Top Speed: 105 mph (169 km/h)
0-60 mph (0-96.5 km/h): 11.4 sec

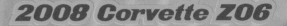

2008 Corvette Z06

Power: 505 hp
Engine Size: 427 ci/7.0L
Engine Type: LS3 V-8
Weight: 3,132 lbs (1,421 kg)
Top Speed: 190 mph (306 km/h)
0-60 mph (0-96.5 km/h): 4.3 sec

GLOSSARY

anniversary The annual celebration of a special event.

concept car A car made to show off a new idea, style, or technology, often first shown at car shows.

convertible A car with a roof that may be lowered or removed.

coupe A smaller, enclosed car that usually seats two people and has a body smaller than that of a sedan.

cylinder The long, rounded chamber in which a piston moves in the engine of a car, providing power. The more cylinders in a motor, the more power it generates.

disk brakes A device for slowing or stopping a car that uses two pads that close around a rounded disk inside the wheel.

exhaust The pipe in the back or on the side of a car through which fumes and smoke are released from a working engine.

fiberglass A product that is made from extremely thin fibers of glass to create a material that can be used many ways, including forming the body of an automobile.

grill The front part of a car, usually made of shiny metal, which protects the engine but also provides a sharp look for the vehicle.

horsepower A measure of the power generated by a motor or engine. The greater the horsepower (hp), the higher the speed at which an automobile is able to travel.

mechanics Professionals who are skilled in making, operating, or repairing machines, especially automobiles.

muscle car The name given to a breed of automobile in the late 1960s and early 1970s that featured a large, powerful engine and bulky frame and was capable of traveling quickly.

pace car	A car that leads the competing race cars through a warm-up lap, but does not take part in the race.
pollute	To make the air impure or unclean by releasing harmful gases, often through the exhaust system of a car.
production line	A method of building a product that involves passing it from one station to another and adding a new part or performing a new task at each stop along the way.
prowling	Moving about secretively as if in search of prey.
sleek	Smooth, shiny, and having a sharp, almost glowing appearance.
stingray	A large ray fish with a whiplike tail that has a sharp spine or spines that can inflict painful wounds.
suspension	The system of springs and other supporting devices that are part of a vehicle's frame.
turbo	An engine that is driven by the pressure created by steam or water moving against the curved part of a drive shaft.

FURTHER INFORMATION

BOOKS

Falconer, Tom. *Complete Corvette: A Model-by-Model History of the American Sports Car.* Glen Ellyn, IL: Crestline Publishing, 2003.

Leffingwell, Randy. *Corvette Fifty Years.* Osceola, WI: Motorbooks International, 2002.

Mueller, Mike. *Corvette 1968–1992.* Osceola, WI: Motorbooks International, 2000.

——. *The Complete Book of Corvette: Every Model Since 1953.* Osceola, WI: Motorbooks International, 2006.

WEB SITES

www.chevrolet.com
www.corvetteimages.com
www.corvettemuseum.com
www.corvetteracing.com

INDEX

Page numbers in **boldface** are photographs.

About the Author

MICHAEL BRADLEY is a writer and broadcaster who lives near Philadelphia. He has written for *Sports Illustrated for Kids, Hoop, Inside Stuff,* and *Slam* magazines and is a regular contributor to Comcast SportsNet in Philadelphia.